Chapter 1

*"Remember, remember
The fifth of November,
Gunpowder, treason and plot."*

We recite these lines at firework parties on 5th November. Sometimes there is a straw Guy to burn on the bonfire, too. But why?

Because, on 5th November 1605, a man called Guy Fawkes and his friends tried to blow up the House of Lords. They wanted to kill King James I.

Guy did not lead the gang. But he played a big part in what happened.

Guy Fawkes was born in April 1570, in York – a big city full of merchants and scholars. It had a very fine cathedral. Christian worshippers prayed there for Elizabeth, their queen. But not all Christians supported Elizabeth.

Christians in England were divided; the Church was split into two main parts. On one side were the Roman Catholics. They believed the head of the Church was the Pope, who ruled from his great Vatican Palace in Rome.

On the other side in England were the Protestants. Queen Elizabeth was their leader. She followed in the footsteps of her father, Henry VIII. He had argued with the Pope about the best way to worship God. He broke away from Rome and set up his own 'Church of England'.

In York – as in the rest of England – Catholics and Protestants lived side by side. But Catholics were afraid of the Queen. She sent them to prison, or fined them, if they did not agree with her Protestant beliefs.

Some priests on the run were executed... if they were found hiding in priest-holes.

So England's Catholics were unhappy. People called them traitors, and the bravest of them began to plot against the Queen.

"We will fight back. Our time will come," they said.

But the Catholics' troubles continued. Things were so bad that in 1587 Elizabeth I's cousin, the Catholic Mary Queen of Scots, was executed for treason.

King Philip of Spain decided to help England's Catholics. He sent a huge Spanish Armada to England. But Elizabeth's navy, led by Sir Francis Drake, scattered the Spanish fleet.

Back in York, despite all these problems, Guy Fawkes made a decision. He would leave his dead father's Protestant religion. "I'll be a Catholic, like my mother and my friends," he said.

Guy Fawkes hoped that King Philip of Spain would try again to help put a Catholic on the English throne – so in 1593 Guy joined the Spanish army then fighting in Flanders (Belgium).

"If I learn about gunpowder, and how to kill rebellious Protestants ... these will be very useful skills!" King Philip of Spain paid Guy Fawkes well for his work. And Guy became known as Guido.

Chapter 2

Back in England there were plots to kill the Queen. The famous Earl of Essex was beheaded for his treachery. John Wright, a school friend of Guy Fawkes, had plotted with Essex. He was lucky to escape with his life.

"The Queen is dying, anyway," thought Wright. "The new King has promised to be fair to Protestants and Catholics. We must wait and see."

In 1603 the old Queen died. "Long live the King!" the people cried, "God save King James I!"

King James was a Protestant, but English Catholics trusted this new king from Scotland.

"He is a wise man. And his mother was Mary Queen of Scots," they said. "A Catholic! He will be fair to us."

But James did not keep his word. "Our King has betrayed us," said the Catholics. One of them, Robert Catesby, was so angry that he started a plot against the King – he had plotted against the old Queen too. He asked his friends, Yorkshiremen Thomas Percy and John Wright, to join him.

"BY HEAVEN WE'LL HATCH ANOTHER PLOT," cried Catesby. "This time we'll KILL the King. And I'll pick our best, truest Catholics to help."

Catesby thought for a moment. "But who?"

He wrote down three names. There was John Wright's brother, Kit, Thomas Wintour, a scholar, traveller and soldier – and finally, John Wright's old schoolfellow, Guy Fawkes.

"We could use a man who works with gunpowder," grinned Catesby.

Thomas Wintour sailed to Flanders to speak to Guy Fawkes. "Guido, come home. Join our fight against the King."

In April 1604, they returned to England together.

In a dark tavern, the plotters sat nervously. Catesby beckoned them over to discuss the plot.

"Guard against spies, my friends. For soon we will kill the King. When he opens Parliament, we will BLOW him to pieces. And his Protestant Lords with him!"

"But how?" asked Thomas Percy.

"Why, we will put gunpowder under the House of Lords, and light the fuse," Catesby replied.

"And then?"

"Then Catholics will rule this land."

"I've rented a house. It's by the House of Lords," Catesby added. "Guy Fawkes, you will be our 'caretaker'. We will dig in the cellar, and tunnel from the house to below their Lordships' Chamber. Then our caretaker will light the gunpowder, and..."

They could imagine the panic.

"The gunpowder must be kept safe till we use it," Guy Fawkes said. Catesby made Robert Keyes its guard. The gang did not see a shadowy figure slip away from the tavern.

Was there really a tunnel?
No one really knows. It would be difficult to keep such a secret.
No one heard any digging...

A few months later Catesby's men met again – at the theatre.

"Good fortune is smiling upon us – I can scarcely believe it," whispered Catesby. "The coal cellar under the House of Lords is empty! The merchants have gone and it's ours to rent!"

Meanwhile, the gang grew to thirteen.

"Can so many keep our plan secret?" thought Guy Fawkes. "And now there's the plague. King James won't open Parliament this year."

Robert Catesby
Thomas Wintour
Robert Wintour
John Wright
Kit Wright
Guy Fawkes.
Thomas Percy
Thomas Bates
Robert Keyes
Francis Tresham
Sir Everard Digby
John Grant
Ambrose Rookwood

Destroy immediately!!

Chapter 3

It was 1605, late October. The gunpowder was ready, safe in Lambeth.

Across London, a letter was brought to Lord Monteagle. It was unsigned.

The letter warned Monteagle to stay away from the opening of Parliament. Monteagle was a Catholic, but loyal to the King. He took the letter to Robert Cecil, the King's most important adviser.

Meanwhile...
"Carefully now!"
Robert Keyes was
loading a boat on the
Thames. He counted thirty-six
barrels of gunpowder, bound
for the House of Lords. First
they had to pass the King's
Guards, then be hidden
under logs in the cellar. It
was easy! Guy, under the
name of 'Mr Johnson',
was left to guard it.

On 4th November 1605, there were shouts in the House of Lords. "SEARCH THE CELLAR, BY ORDER OF THE KING," cried a guard.

"We're betrayed!" Guy thought as he scuttled into the shadows.

At much the same time, King James was reading Monteagle's letter again.

"It seems they mean violence, my Lord Cecil," he said.

"I think you may be right, Your Majesty," replied his adviser.

My Lord out of the love i beare to some of youer frends I have a caer of youer preservation.

26th October in the year of our Lord 1605. Lord Monteagle. Avoid attending Parliament. Those that do shall receive a terrible blow.

In the cellar, Guy watched the noisy guards leave.

"Nothing here!" they shouted. "Just that tall and desperate fellow. A servant I'd say."

Guy thanked God for his lucky escape, and he stayed out of sight.

Just a tall and desperate fellow.

Who wrote to Lord Monteagle? Was it one of the plotters? Or a government spy, who had watched them for months?

Why hadn't Robert Cecil done anything about the letter earlier? Did he hope to catch more of the gang? It seems he and the King had known about the plot all along – but now it was time to act.

It was just before midnight on 4th November.

In the cold, dark, cellar, lantern-light picked out the scuttling rats.

Very soon King James's Parliament would meet above the deadly gunpowder store.

Guy was ready to light the fuse – his role in the plot.

"When I light this, the King will be blown to bits!" he laughed. "England will be Catholic in a blink of an eye."

"BANG!!"

The doors burst open!

Guy panicked. "Who told the guards?"

In a muddle of footsteps and shouts, they grabbed him. Soldiers rushed straight to the woodpile.

"GUNPOWDER!" they exclaimed.

Chapter 4

At about 4 o'clock in the morning of 5th November, Guy was dragged in to the King's Chamber. His hands were bound. He was frightened.

"Your name?" thundered the King. "Are you a Catholic? Answer now, or be sorry!"

Even after two days, Guy told them nothing about the plot. "My name is John Johnson. I am working alone," he said.

"TAKE HIM TO THE TOWER!" raged the King. "The rack will loosen his tongue!"

It took two days of torture before Guy cried out, "STOP NOW! I am Guido Fawkes.

I will give you the names of my friends."

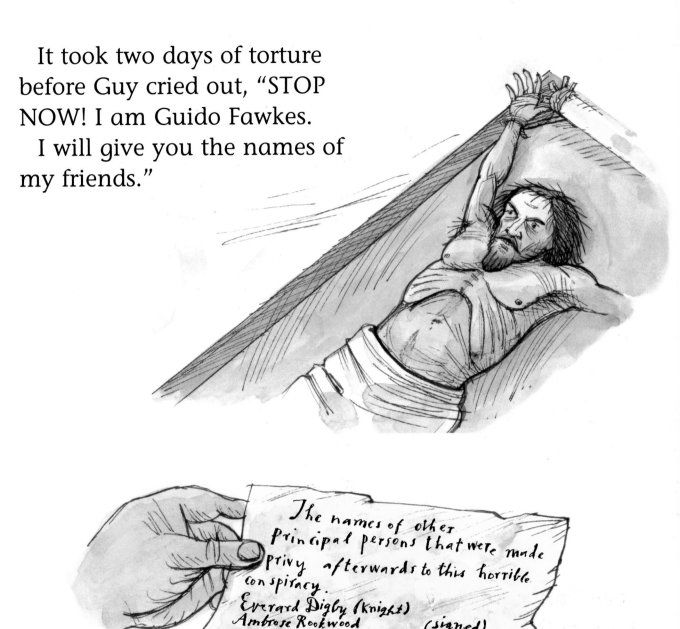

The names of other Principal persons that were made privy afterwards to this horrible conspiracy.

Everard Digby (knight)
Ambrose Rookwood
Francis Tresham
John Grant
Robert Keyes Wintour

(signed)
Guido Fawkes
Eg wid.

"Find these men, and bring them to the Tower!" the King ordered his guards.

25

Catesby had fled to the Midlands with some of his men. But their gunpowder was wet. They had only swords for defence.

As the King's men surrounded their house, Catesby shouted, "We'll make our stand here! Dry the powder, and prepare to fight!"

"BOOM!!" Gunpowder exploded by an open fire, blinding John Grant.

"OPEN FIRE!" Musket-fire whistled and thudded into Holbeach House, and the Wrights died. A single bullet killed Catesby and Percy.

Only eight survivors were brought to Westminster Hall, for a very short trial. Finally, the judge spoke.

"We have found you guilty of treason. You will suffer a traitor's death.

At your place of execution you will be hung by the neck, taken down alive, and cut to pieces."

On 30th January 1606, Robert Wintour, Sir Everard Digby, blind John Grant and Thomas Bates were executed. They were followed the next day by Thomas Wintour, Ambrose Rookwood, Robert Keyes and, last of all, Guy Fawkes – the plotter we remember.

Their heads were stuck on spikes, and birds pecked at their dead faces.

In the end King James was safe – and his country united against the Catholic cause. Was that what King James and Robert Cecil wanted all along?

Catholics and Protestants still feared one another and did so for a long time to come. But today everybody enjoys the bonfires and fireworks on 5th November.

Timeline

1534 Henry VIII is named Head of the Church of England. England's break from the Pope in Rome complete.

1547 Henry VIII dies. His young son Edward VI becomes King.

1553 Edward dies. His Catholic half-sister Mary becomes queen. She reunites the English Church with the Roman Catholic Church.

1558 Mary dies. Elizabeth I, a Protestant, becomes queen. The Church of England breaks again from the Roman Catholic Church.

1570 Guy Fawkes is born in York.

1577 Sir Francis Drake begins his 3-year voyage around the world.

1579 Guy's father, Edward Fawkes, dies.

1581 Guy's mother, Edith, remarries a Catholic, Denis Bainbridge.
The Dutch declare independence from Spain, leading to war.

1587 Mary Queen of Scots beheaded.

1588 The Spanish Armada defeated by the English navy – and bad weather.

1592 Guy goes to fight against the Dutch for Catholic Spain.

1599 The Globe Theatre opens in London. Shakespeare's plays are staged there.

1601 The Earl of Essex is executed for treason.

1603 Elizabeth dies and is succeeded by her cousin James VI of Scotland; now King James I of England.

1604 April Guy Fawkes returns to England to join Catesby's plot.

Autumn Parliament not called because of plague in London.

1605 26th October Lord Monteagle gets a warning letter and takes it to Cecil.

30th October Gunpowder now in cellars beneath Parliament.

4th November First, unsuccessful, search of the cellars.

4–5th November Gunpowder found and Guy is arrested.

8th November Rest of plotters either shot or captured.

1606 29–30th January Guy and other captured plotters are executed.

1606 Parliament declares 5th November a national day of thanksgiving and people celebrate with bonfires.

Quiz

Can you remember?

1. Why did Guy Fawkes want to blow up the House of Lords?

2. Who did the Roman Catholics believe was the Head of the Church?

3. Was Guy Fawkes a Catholic or a Protestant when he plotted to kill the King?

4. What was Guy's nickname?

5. Why was Guy Fawkes chosen to help with the plot?

6. What was Guy Fawkes supposed to do in the plot?

7. How many barrels of gunpowder were to be used?

8. How many people were involved in the plot?

9. Who did Guy Fawkes claim he was when he was caught?

10. What happened to the people who were involved in the plot?

11. What do people do today to celebrate 5th November?

Answers on page 32

Glossary

armada A large group of war ships.

execute To kill someone as a punishment.

fuse The length of material which is burnt to make gunpowder explode.

plague Deadly disease caught by humans from rat-fleas.

plot A secret plan, usually against the law.

rack A machine used to torture people by stretching them.

rebellious Describes someone who seeks to rebel or go against the rulers of a country.

torture Hurting someone, often very badly, in order to punish them or make them admit to a crime.

traitor A person who does something which damages or betrays their country or the rulers of their country.

treachery The actions of a traitor.

treason Trying to damage or overthrow the rulers of a country.

trial A hearing to decide if a person has broken the law.

Index

Quiz answers

1. To kill the King (James I)
2. The Pope
3. Catholic
4. Guido
5. Because he worked with gunpowder.
6. Tunnel from the house to the House of Lords and light the gunpowder.
7. 36
8. 13
9. John Johnson
10. They were executed
11. Light bonfires and set off fireworks